BEYOND THE THEORY: SCIENCE OF THE FUTURE

IS HUMAN CLONING IN OUR FUTURE?

THEORIES ABOUT GENETICS

Tom Jackson

Gareth Stevens PUBLISHING

Please visit our website, www.garethstevens.com.
For a free color catalog of all our high-quality books,
call toll free 1-800-542-2595 or fax 1-877-542-2596.

Cataloging-in-Publication Data

Names: Jackson, Tom.
Title: Is human cloning in our future? theories about genetics / Tom Jackson.
Description: New York : Gareth Stevens Publishing, 2019. | Series: Beyond the theory: science of the future | Includes glossary and index.
Identifiers: LCCN ISBN 9781538226711 (pbk.) | ISBN 9781538226704 (library bound)
Subjects: LCSH: Genes--Juvenile literature. | Human genetics--Juvenile literature. | Human cloning--Juvenile literature.
Classification: LCC QH447.J33 2019 | DDC 572.8'6--dc23

First Edition

Published in 2019 by
Gareth Stevens Publishing
111 East 14th Street, Suite 349
New York, NY 10003

Produced for Gareth Stevens by Calcium
Editors: Sarah Eason and Tim Cooke
Designers: Emma DeBanks and Lynne Lennon
Picture researcher: Rachel Blount

Picture credits: Cover: Shutterstock: Kentoh: foreground, The Biochemist Artist: background; Inside: Shutterstock: Scisetti Alfio: p. 14; Roongrote Amnuaysook: p. 21; Andrey_Popov: p. 28; Esteban De Armas: p. 35; Blackboard: p. 16; Everett Historical: pp. 5, 36; FloridaStock: pp. 28-29t; Gopixa: p. 39; Igorstevanovic: p. 38; Jjustas: p. 31r; Victor Josan: pp. 30-31t; Sebastian Kaulitzki: p. 9t; Kerale: p. 13t; Robert Kneschke: p. 22; Kateryna Kon: p. 6; Dan Bach Kristensen: p. 26; David Litman: p. 33; Lopolo: pp. 8-9; Maxim Maksutov: p. 34; Frances van der Merwe: p. 7; Levgenii Meyer: p. 4; Molekuul_b: p. 40; Mopic: p. 43; Vladimir Mulder: p. 24; Petarg: p. 41; Chai Seamaker: p. 23; Viewimage: p. 10; Andrii Vodolazhskyi: pp. 20, 32; Vrx: p. 42; WhiteMocca: p. 37; Wichy: p. 17; YuriyZhuravov: pp. 1, 12-13b; Wikimedia Commons: p. 15; Maggie Bartlett, NHGRI: p. 25; C-M: p. 27; Biswarup Ganguly: p. 19; Neverbutterfly: p. 11; James Tourtellotte, photo editor of CBP Today: p. 18.

Printed in the United States of America

CPSIA compliance information: Batch #CS18GS:
For further information contact Gareth Stevens, New York, New York at 1-800-542-2595.

CONTENTS

CHAPTER 1

GENETICS AND CLONES

Genetics is the study of how information about how to build a new body is transmitted from parents to their offspring. This process is called inheritance. Genetics is a relatively new science, but the ideas behind it have been known since early times. Although the word "genetics" itself is only about 100 years old, humans have been exploiting the science of genetics for the last 10,000 years.

Early farmers tried to grow types of wheat that were easier to harvest.

Our ancient ancestors understood that children shared some of the features of their parents. They noticed that the same was true for plants and animals. People used this knowledge to create the first crops, using plants such as wheat and rice. Wild wheat plants drop their grains to the ground in a process called shattering. A light knock makes all the seeds fall from the stalk so they will get a chance to sprout into new plants. Early humans had to pick up the seeds one by one to eat. Sometimes, however, our ancestors found wheat plants that did not shatter. Instead, all the grains stayed on the plant. This made them easier to harvest. Early farmers chose the seeds of these grains to plant to grow entire fields of this useful wheat.

Today, the bread we eat is still made from the grains of the very same plants. Farmers selected only the useful wheat to grow, which then produced more plants that did not shatter. Eventually, all wheat kept its seeds on the plant. The way the grains of a plant behave is a genetic trait, or characteristic, meaning that it is inherited. By preferring some plants over others, early farmers were controlling the genes of their crops. Genes are the biological units that carry information from a parent to its offspring. Over the centuries, farmers used the same technique to breed many varieties of food plants and farm animals. They did not know it, but our ancestors were modifying or engineering the genetics of these organisms. Today, scientists know a great deal more about how genes work. They can modify the genes of any living thing—even humans. But would that be a useful thing to do? To find out, we need to go beyond the theory.

By the time of the ancient Egyptians, domesticated wheat was a major crop.

WHAT IS A CLONE?

Every living body is made of building blocks called cells. Some basic forms of life have only a single cell. A human body contains about 37 billion cells. It begins with a single cell called a zygote. The zygote divides and multiplies. Eventually the cells make a new body with organs, senses, limbs, and all the features it needs to survive.

This development is controlled by a set of instructions, called genes. A gene is a piece of a chemical called deoxyribonucleic acid, known as DNA. DNA is physically moved from one generation to the next. It is transported from the parents' cells to their offsprings' zygotes.

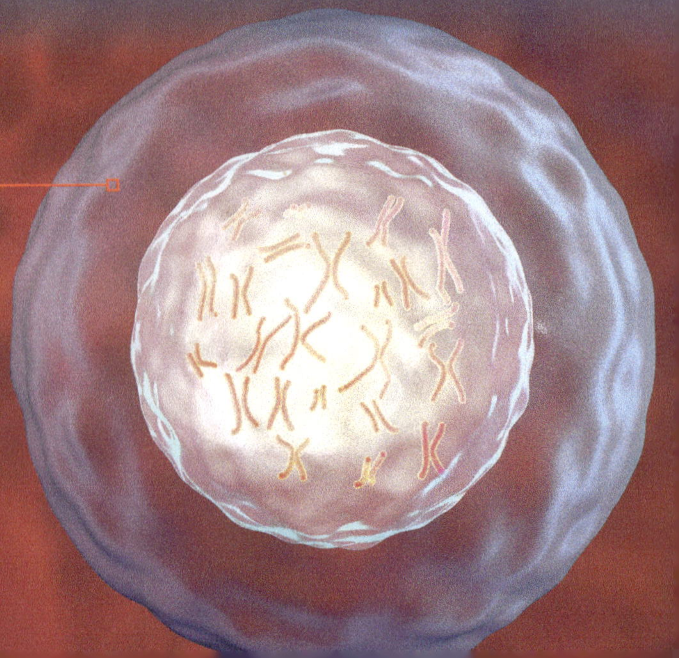

This illustration shows the tiny structures that carry DNA inside the cells of all living bodies.

UNANSWERED

Across the natural world, most animals reproduce sexually. They create offspring using cells from both a mother and a father. However, some **species** reproduce **asexually**, so offspring only have a mother. Offspring produced asexually have an identical set of genes to their mother, making them genetic **clones**. Scientists create clones asexually, but it is difficult. Will it ever become as straightforward as asexual reproduction in the natural world?

Female aphids give birth to live young without needing cells from a male. This allows the population to grow rapidly.

DNA is quite fragile and easily damaged. It is packaged and protected inside stronger structures called **chromosomes**. Nearly every cell in any body contains the same full set of chromosomes.

In humans and other animals, such as birds and mammals, each individual has a unique set of genes in their chromosomes. Half of the genes came from their mother and the other half from their father. In species that reproduce asexually, offspring have identical genes to their mother only, making them clones (see box). Geneticists—scientists who study genes—have learned to reorganize the way zygotes are created in sexual animals. They can create animals in the laboratory that have identical genes to their mothers only. These animals are clones. So far, no human clone has been made this way. Even so, there are already plenty of human clones around. We know them better as identical twins.

NATURAL CLONES

About 1.5 percent of the human population is a twin. Of those twins, about four out of every five pairs of twins are described as fraternal. That means they just happened to develop inside their mother at the same time. They are no more closely related than any other brother and sister. Their genes are similar, but they do not match perfectly.

The rarer kind of twins are identical twins. Identical twins grow up to look so similar that people will struggle to be able to tell them apart. The twins appear so similar because they have identical sets of genes. In other words, they are clones of each other.

Identical twins are sometimes called monozygotic twins, because they come from a single zygote.

UNANSWERED

Identical twins are often the subject of research. Researchers try to discover what impact environment has on their development. Environmental factors include things such as the twins' diet, illnesses, and any injuries they suffer. Twin research may also reveal how much genetics affect hard-to-measure features such as intelligence and personality. Identical twins always have the same genes, but do they always have the same personalities?

Identical twins are produced through the same system of sexual reproduction that creates any other baby. The process begins with the parents producing **sex cells**. Male sex cells are known as sperm and female sex cells as eggs. Sex cells differ from other body cells because they have only half the number of chromosomes as regular body cells. Human sperm and eggs have 23 chromosomes each. When a sperm and an egg merge to make a zygote, that zygote has a full set of 46 chromosomes.

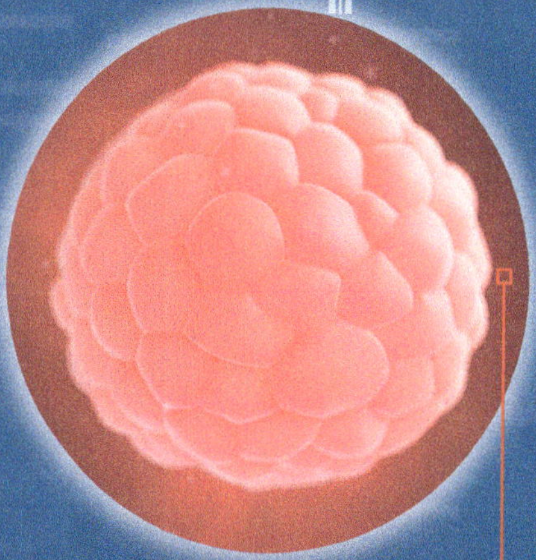

Identical twins are created when the ball of cells created by the zygote splits in two.

The zygote then starts to divide into a ball of cells. This group of cells, the **blastocyst**, goes on to become a new human body. Sometimes, during the first 12 days of its existence, the blastocyst spontaneously splits into two balls. Each of these balls continues to develop independently within the mother—forming identical individuals. (Although it is very rare in humans, sometimes the split happens again and even a third time. This produces identical triplets or quadruplets.)

DOLLY THE SHEEP

Identical twins are clones that form in the very earliest stages of their lives. Scientists have learned to make artificial clones from animals that are already fully grown. The first large animal to be cloned in this way was Dolly, a sheep born in 1996. It took three adult female sheep—ewes—to create the clone, so Dolly had three "mothers."

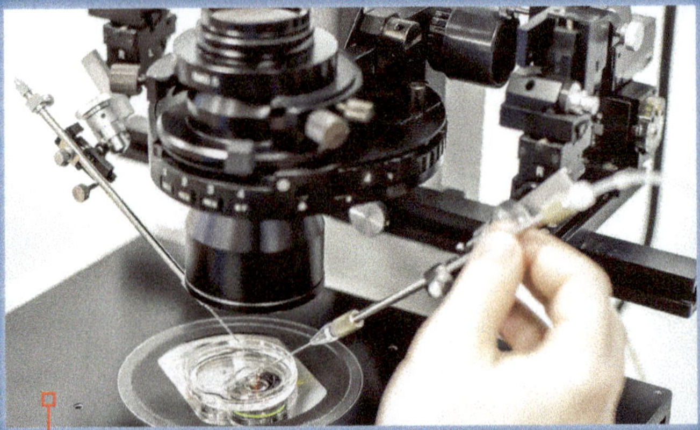

Scientists use powerful microscopes as they modify cells in the laboratory.

The first ewe provided the genetic material. Scientists took a cell from her udder. They removed the nucleus, which is the central part of the cell that contains the chromosomes. Next, they took an egg cell from a second ewe. As a sex cell, this egg had only a half set of chromosomes. The scientists removed the chromosomes and put the nucleus from the first sheep in their place. This turned the egg into a zygote, a single sheep cell with a full set of chromosomes. (Not all DNA is contained in the nucleus of a cell. Some exists outside of the nucleus, in structures called **mitochondria**. Dolly's mitochondria carried genes from Mother Two, meaning she was not strictly a complete clone of Mother One.)

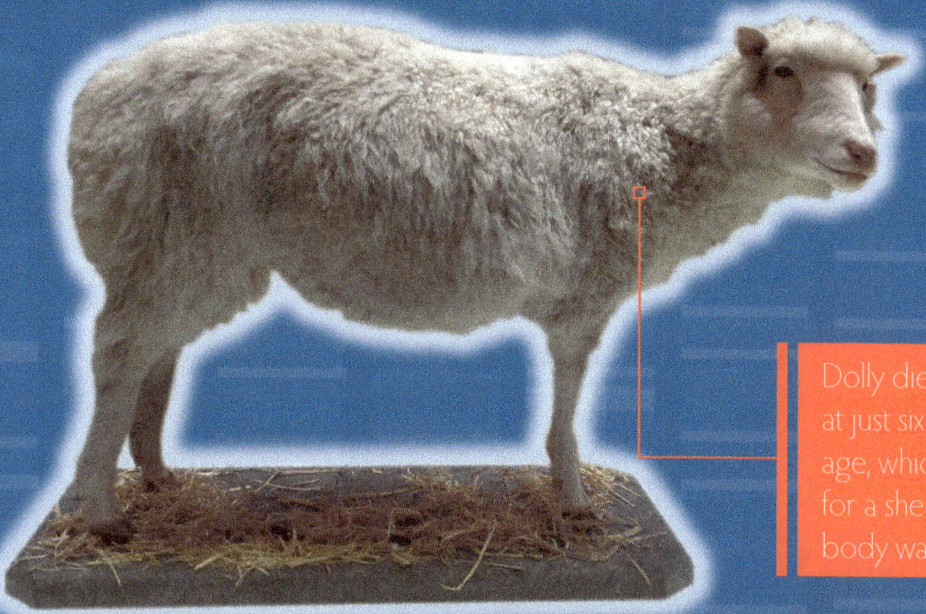

Dolly died in 2003 at just six years of age, which is young for a sheep. Her body was preserved.

Dolly's zygote was not able to divide and multiply naturally. The researchers in Scotland who created Dolly gave the zygote a tiny electric shock to kick-start the process. The cells began to divide and multiply. The scientists then placed the growing blastocyst in the **uterus** of a third sheep. It developed as a normal baby sheep, resulting about four months later in Dolly—the most famous sheep in history.

UNANSWERED

Dolly suffered from arthritis, a joint problem usually associated with older animals. This led researchers to suggest that Dolly had aged prematurely. They wondered if the problem was caused because she inherited "old" chromosomes from her mother. However, in 2007, four healthy clones were born using cells taken from the same mother, at the same time. Dolly probably became sick because she lived indoors—but no one knows for sure.

COULD WE CLONE A HUMAN?

Dolly the Sheep was cloned by taking a cell nucleus from an animal and using it to make a new zygote. This process is called nuclear transfer. It has been used to clone horses, cats, cows, and other familiar animals. It might help to boost the numbers of animal species threatened with extinction. So why has no one cloned a human yet?

One answer is that nuclear transfer is not easy. Although no one knows why, it is particularly difficult to clone **primates**, such as monkeys, apes, and humans, in this way. The process is very expensive, because it frequently goes wrong. It took 277 failed cloning attempts before Dolly was created. Many of those attempts got a long way before they failed.

Books and movies often depict clones as instant copies of a person—but that's not how it works.

They usually failed because of complications in the way lambs developed inside their mothers. Researchers decided that the suffering of the lambs was worth it to unlock the secrets of cloning. No one thinks that similar risks to human babies are worth taking.

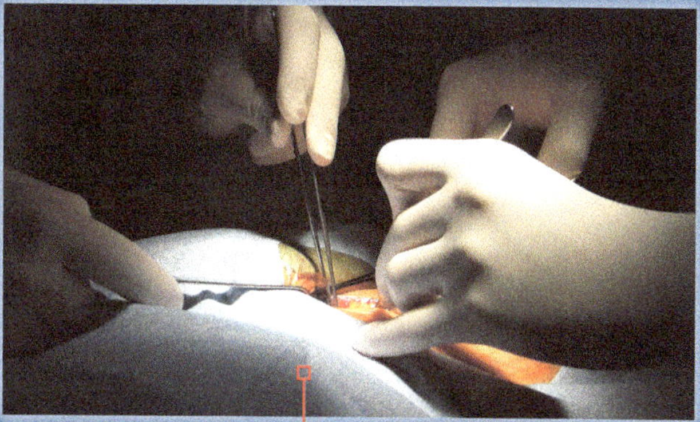

One possible use for clones would be to provide organs for transplantation.

Other **ethical** problems relate to the possible purposes of human cloning. One suggestion is that we could clone our dead relatives; another is to grow a new body for harvesting organs for **transplantation**. Will it ever be okay to create a new person for these kinds of reasons? Would a clone benefit from being brought to life, or would it only exist for someone else's purposes? Science-fiction movies give the impression that a human clone is an instant copy of a person. In fact, a clone is a baby that might grow up to look a lot like their "parent"—but that will always be a completely different individual, with unique memories and experiences.

UNANSWERED

Some people believe that a zygote is a human being with the same rights as any living person. However, others, including cloning scientists, have a different view. Many zygotes never become humans, so the cell never becomes part of a body. The first evidence of a human body is a line of cells called the primitive strip. It appears after 15 days of development. For that reason, researchers are allowed to experiment with human blastocysts for 14 days, but no longer.

CHAPTER 2

GENETICS AT WORK

The most precise definition of a gene is that it is the unit of inheritance—the thing that moves from one generation to the next. But what is that "thing"? Although the word gene was first used in 1909, the idea is a little older. In the 1850s, a Czech monk named Gregor Mendel experimented with pea plants to find out how inheritance worked. Although he used other terms to describe what he found, his work formed the basis of modern genetics. It was further confirmed by the later discovery of chromosomes and DNA.

Gregor Mendel studied the colors of pea plants to figure out how inheritance worked.

Every body cell contains not one but two copies of each gene. Each gene has a number of varieties, which are known as **alleles**. For example, the gene for eye color has brown, blue, gray, green, and hazel alleles. During reproduction, each parent contributes one allele to their offspring. This makes a new double set of alleles in the zygote. In each pair of alleles, one is dominant and the other is recessive, or weaker.

The set of alleles in the zygote—and every body cell that grows from it—is called the **genotype**. To take a simple example, say that the allele for brown eyes is B and blue eyes is b. There are four possible genotypes from the pairs of alleles: BB, Bb, bB, and bb. Under the control of the genotype, the body develops an inherited feature that can be observed, called a **phenotype**. Because the B allele is dominant, the first three genotypes above produce a brown-eye phenotype. Whenever someone inherits B, they will have brown eyes. They only get blue eyes if they inherit two bs.

This gives us two ways of understanding what a gene is. It could be a phenotype, a characteristic that can be measured, such as eye color, or it could be a genotype, a physical piece of DNA that exists inside cells. The primary goal of geneticists is to figure out how the two ideas of a gene are linked. How do the pieces of DNA make a body?

There are six colors of human eye: blue, brown, gray, hazel, amber, and red.

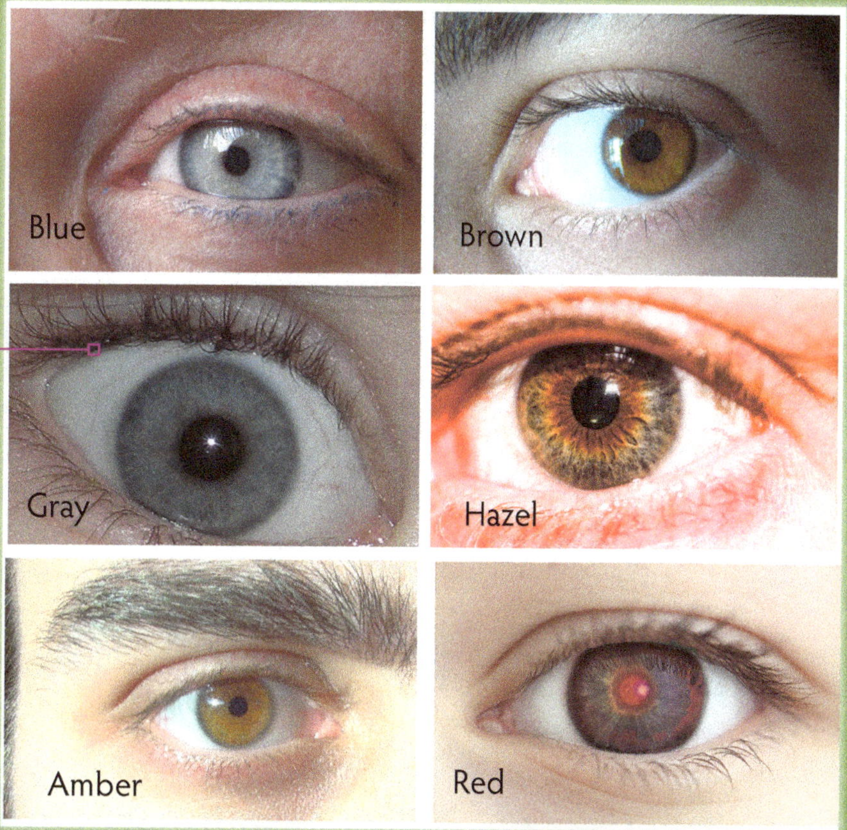

DNA

As the name deoxyribonucleic acid suggests, DNA is a complex molecule. DNA is a double helix, or spiral, of molecules that can reach enormous lengths. Every cell in the body carries over 6.5 feet (2 m) of DNA. The DNA from a whole body joined together would reach to the sun and back almost four times!

DNA is usually pictured as a twisting ladder. The deoxyribose part of its name refers to sugar molecules that form two long chains on the outer edge of the molecule. The rungs of the ladder are formed by nucleic acids known as bases. DNA uses four types of base: adenine, thymine, guanine, and cytosine. Each rung of the DNA ladder is made up of a pair of bases. Adenine always pairs with thymine and guanine with cytosine. A DNA molecule is formed from two strands linked in the middle by rungs, with each strand being a kind of mirror image of the other.

The most common depiction shows DNA as a twisting ladder or spiral.

BEHIND THE THEORY

DNA was first isolated by Friedrich Miescher, a Swiss doctor, in 1871. Although its role in genetics was confirmed in the 1940s, no one knew how it carried information. In 1952, researchers used new techniques to image the complex shape of the DNA molecule. Rosalind Franklin analyzed an image to discover key features of DNA molecules. The Cambridge researchers, James Watson and Francis Crick, used that information to figure out the double helix structure in 1953, and later figured out the coding system.

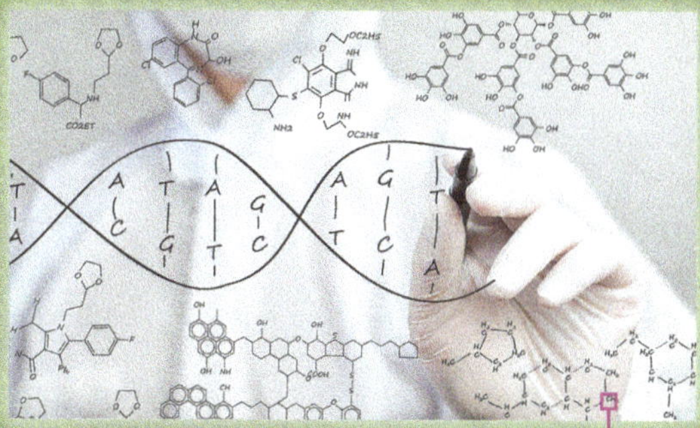

The four bases form rungs between the longer sugar molecules of DNA.

Scientists give each base one of the following letters: ATGC. One strand of the DNA might have this sequence of bases: TAGCAT. The opposite strand would therefore have the sequence ATCGTA. In total, human DNA has 3 billion of these base pairs, which create a long code of the four bases. This code carries the specific instructions for many thousands of genes. The structure of DNA and its code were revealed in the 1950s, and the decoding began.

READING THE CHEMICAL CODE

The DNA code is a set of instructions for how to build proteins. Proteins are tiny cellular machines that do all the jobs of life. A human body uses about 10,000 different proteins. Every one of these proteins is coded by a section of human DNA called a cistron. (The information on a cistron travels only from the DNA to the cell, never the other way around.)

A protein is made up of around 100 smaller units called amino acids. There are about 20 of these acids, which are put together in chains. The precise sequence of the amino acid chain defines the shape of the finished protein—and that shape defines what job the protein can do.

A scientist studies a genetic profile on a piece of film.

UNANSWERED

In 2003 the complete human **genome**—a list of human genetic material—was decoded. The result was more than 3 billion characters in the ATGC code, which filled 130 printed books. It would take 95 years to read aloud. However, by itself the list was useless, so since 2003 geneticists have been searching for genes among all the data. Not all DNA carries a genetic code. Geneticists estimate that 70 percent of the human genome is junk DNA!

An exhibit in a museum in India celebrates the decoding of the human genome.

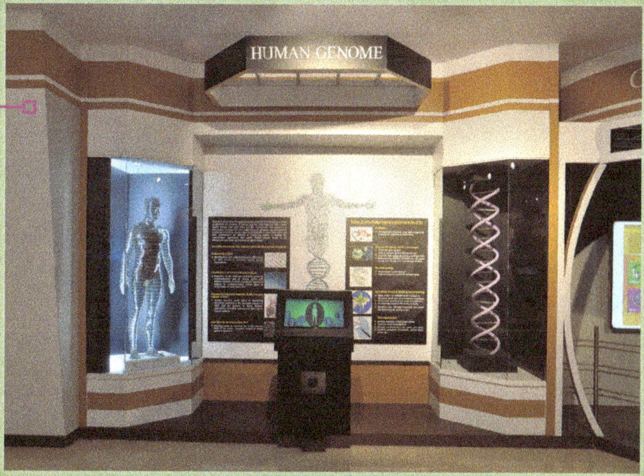

Turning DNA into protein is a complex process. It begins with the double helix "unzipping" into two strands. One carries the DNA code, while the other becomes a template, or pattern, for a copy called messenger RNA (mRNA). RNA, or ribonucleic acid, is similar to DNA, but it can exist as a single strand rather than a double helix.

The mRNA leaves the nucleus and travels to a protein factory called a **ribosome**, where it is fed through three bases at a time. Each three-letter code relates to a particular amino acid. It pulls the right amino acids into position in the protein. The mRNA then shifts to the next three-letter code, and the next amino acid is added. This process is repeated until a brand-new, very precisely structured protein is completed.

STEM CELLS

The cell of any organism contains the full instructions to make a body. However, a body is not just a ball of cells that grows from a zygote. Instead it is made up of a series of systems, such as the nerves and digestive system. Each body system employs a series of organs, which are structures with specific functions. For example, the heart pumps blood and the eyes detect light. In turn, an organ is made from a collection of tissues, which are masses of cells that perform one particular task. For example, muscle tissue is used to provide motion, such as making the heart pump and the eyes swivel.

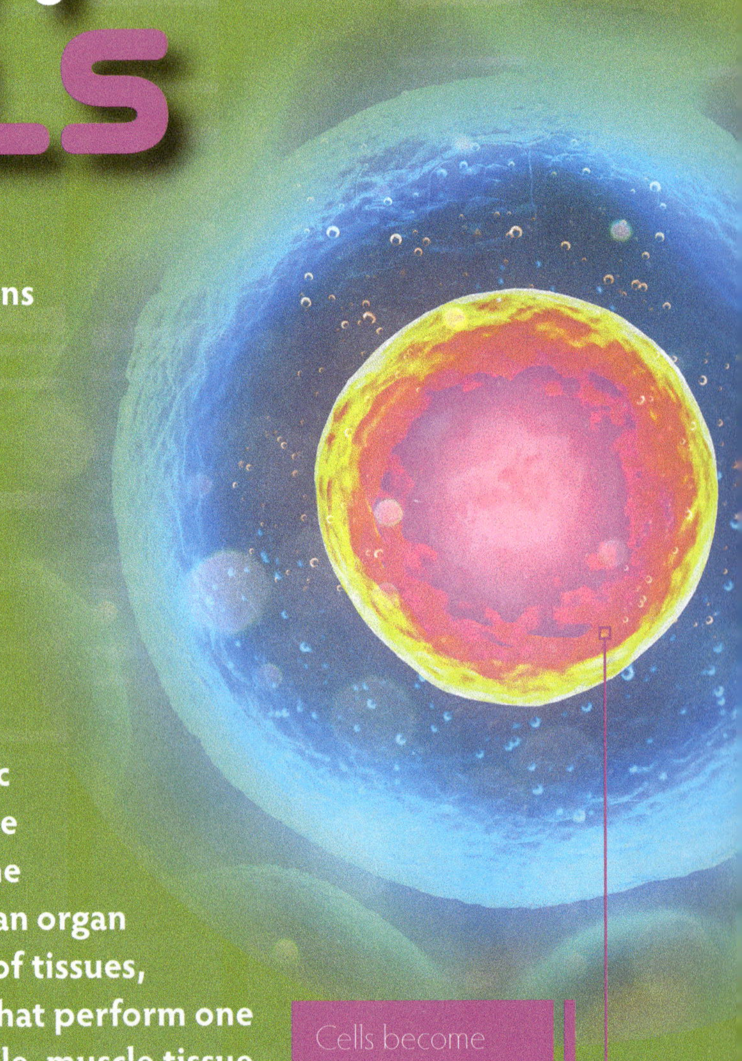

Cells become more specialized in the roles they play in the body.

As the body grows, its cells must specialize. They become different from one another and form tissues that build into organs and body systems. This complex process is controlled using so-called stem cells.

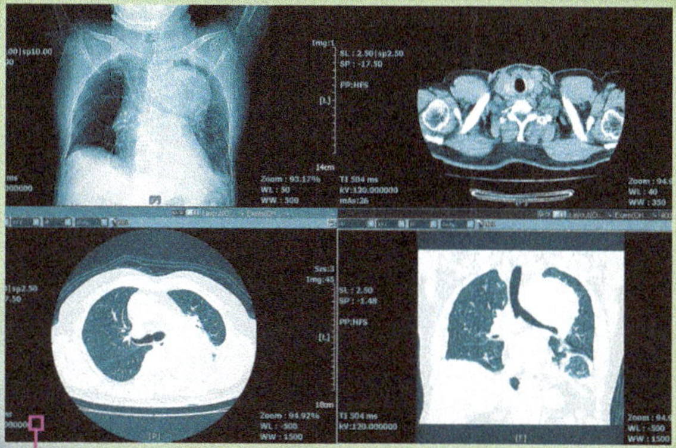

Within the body, such as inside this chest, cells become part of particular organs or tissues.

The zygote and the first few cells in the body can divide and **differentiate** into any type of cell. As they differentiate, cells become less **potent**. The first stage, called pluripotent cells, build the inner, middle, or outer layers of the body. A pluripotent cell can specialize further as one of several multipotent cells, which create cells of a particular tissue type. For example, a middle-layer pluripotent cell can make multipotent cells such as muscle or blood tissue. A blood stem cell then differentiates into red and white blood cells. Each step in the process is irreversible. Once a cell becomes a certain type, it cannot go back to forming a more potent cell. Although the same genes are inside, most are now switched off.

UNANSWERED

During growth, the body's cells divide rapidly under the control of a set of genes. Once the body or a particular part of it is fully grown, the genes controlling it become less active. If they do turn on, and cells start to divide again, the cells self-destruct. However, sometimes the process goes wrong, and the cells continue to divide. As they grow, they form a cancerous **tumor**, which can interfere with the normal functions of the body. We still do not know how to keep cancerous tumors from developing. Understanding how growth genes malfunction is one of the ways doctors hope to fight cancers.

HOX GENES

The development of a body is a remarkable process. Over an average lifespan, a human body undergoes 10,000 trillion cell divisions. Most of those occur in the early stages of life, as the body grows. However, the map of the body—what shape an organism takes— is controlled by a handful of instructions, known as Hox genes.

The human body is shaped so that the right and left halves mirror each other.

Humans are **bilaterally symmetrical**. If a human was sliced down the middle from head to foot and folded in half, the left side would be a mirror image of the right side. The arms, legs, eyes, and other internal and external features are arranged equally on both sides. The Hox genes define where in the body these symmetrical structures will grow, so that an arm matches an arm and a leg matches a leg.

Most animals share a bilateral body plan with humans. Only organisms such as jellyfish and sponges do not. That means the same Hox genes control the growth of worms and whales, fish and flies, and hippos and humans.

UNANSWERED

Some of the most ancient animals, such as insects and worms, had no hard bones to form stony remains called fossils. Researchers are trying to figure out when different types of such animals evolved by using what is called the molecular clock. They compare the genomes of different animals to see how different they are, and estimate how long such genetic differences took to appear. The scientists use the information to figure out when species first appeared.

Hox genes divide the body up into segments, so that limbs or appendages develop at particular points along the body. The alleles of the Hox genes vary from animal to animal, so a millipede develops hundreds of legs, while a dolphin has one set of flippers, and a snake has no appendages at all.

The discovery of the Hox genes and other genetic control systems led to the field of evolutionary developmental biology. Researchers study how different organisms develop as embryos to understand how similar their genes are. The more similar the genes, the more closely related the animals are.

Jellyfish lack the kind of regular shape shared by most animals.

CHAPTER 3

GENETIC MODIFICATION

Genes are always changing as species reproduce. As well as being jumbled up at random during reproduction, genes can also mutate, or change. A mutation is a change in the gene's code, perhaps by changing one "letter" in its sequence of bases, or perhaps by mistakenly copying in an extra chunk of letters. Most mutations result in a protein not working, causing the cell and organism to die. However, some mutations do not lead to death. Instead they result in a new phenotype not previously seen in a species, such as orange eyes or blue hair.

Researchers use genetic changes to create plants with qualities such as the ability to live in dry regions.

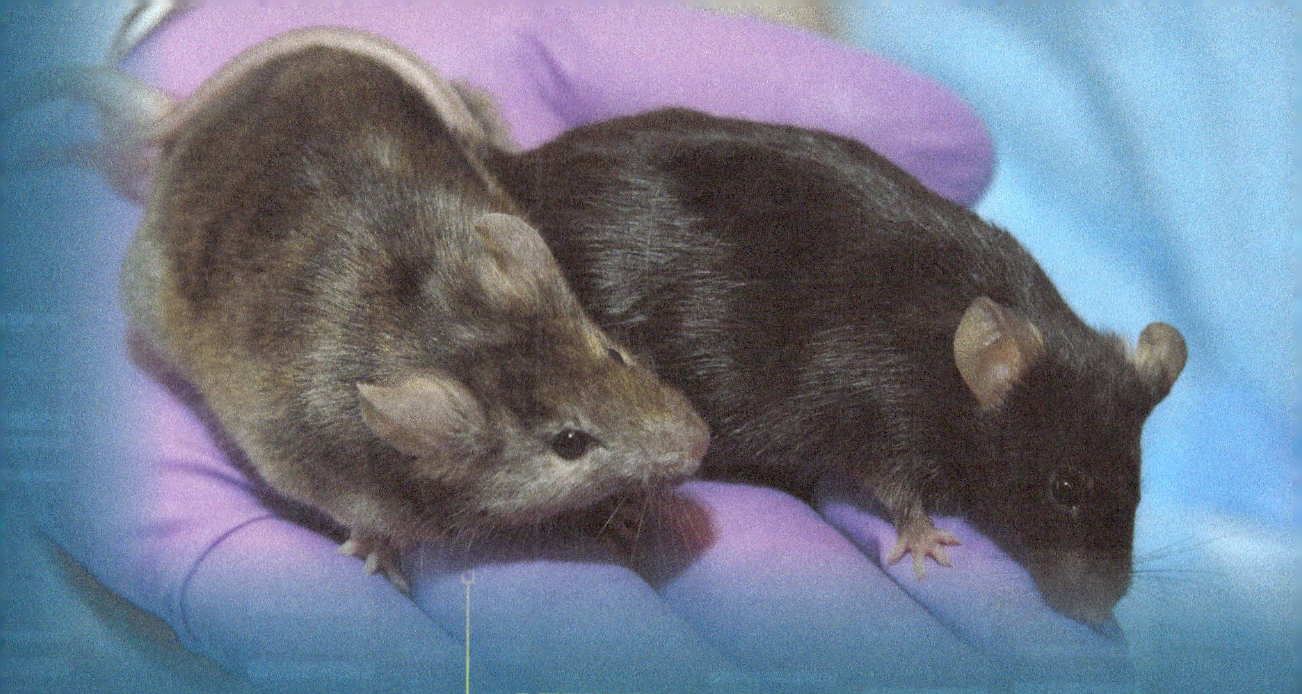

This mouse (left) has been created in a lab to have shorter hair than normal mice (right).

Variations created by genetic mutations drive **natural selection**, which leads to evolution. The mutations that help an organism survive and reproduce become more common than those that hinder survival. Humans have altered the genes of plants and animals using a similar system of artificial selection. That began with the earliest farmers choosing the most useful plants and animals and using them to create new breeds that produce more food, milk, or fur, or strength for labor or transportation.

However, creating organisms by relying on natural mutations and breeding takes many generations—and a long time. In theory, it might be possible to breed a jellyfish into a mouse or a mouse that glows in the dark like a jellyfish, but it would take millions of years. The process has been speeded up by genetic modification technology. Genetic engineering allows scientists to take genes from one organism and add them to the genome of another—which could include putting the genes for glowing proteins into a mouse so it glows in the dark.

GENETIC ENGINEERING

Genetic engineers transfer genes from one organism into a target species. For example, Arctic fish have antifreeze chemicals that prevent them from freezing to death in icy water. In the 1990s, scientists transferred the gene for the antifreeze chemicals to tomatoes, to keep them from being damaged by frosts. It was an amazing technological achievement—even though it did not actually work.

The first stage of the process is to isolate the genetic material from the original species. This is done using chemical tools called recombinant enzymes. These proteins manage the copying and repair of DNA in the nucleus. Scientists use them to boost the numbers of specific genes.

The Arctic char has a natural antifreeze that allows it to live in freezing water.

BEHIND THE THEORY

One of the first genetic engineers was the German biologist Rudolf Jaenisch. In 1974, Jaenisch injected a virus into a mouse embryo, adding a new gene to create the first genetically engineered animal. The new gene was contained inside every one of the mouse's cells. However, the mouse did not pass the new gene on to its offspring. That problem was not fixed until 1981.

Next, the gene needs to be added to the target organism, which is often a simple animal called a bacterium. The simplest technique is to blast the targets with a gene gun. This is an air-powered pistol that fires tiny particles of gold coated with the donor gene. The particles smash into the living cells. They destroy most of the cells, but a few penetrate cells without damaging them. Once the gene is inside, the cell will incorporate it with its own DNA. Plants are genetically engineered using Agrobacterium, a bacterium that infects their cells. Genetic engineers use the bacterium to add a different gene to the plant. Other genes are folded inside artificial infections, which are then used to infect a target.

Agrobacterium is used to add genes to the cells of plants.

GMOs

A GMO is a genetically modified organism. In theory, genetic engineers modify any organism, but they are controlled by strict laws. Some people worry that GMOs made in laboratories might escape into the wild. Their altered genetics might damage wildlife, with irreversible results.

Despite such concerns, GMOs have been used for a range of purposes. The most significant is pharming, in which organisms are used to grow medicines, or pharmaceuticals. For example, people who suffer from the condition of diabetes have an inability to control the level of sugar in their blood. They often have to inject themselves with insulin, a **hormone** that carries out that task. In the past, this insulin came from horses and other large mammals. It did not work very well, and sufferers had to test their blood and inject large amounts each day.

In the 1990s, the human gene for insulin was added to a bacterium called *E. coli*, which is most familiar for causing a nasty type of food poisoning. The genetically modified (GM) strain of this bacterium is now grown in significant amounts in order to produce pure human insulin. This insulin is extracted for use in treating diabetes. It is much more effective than the previous animal insulin.

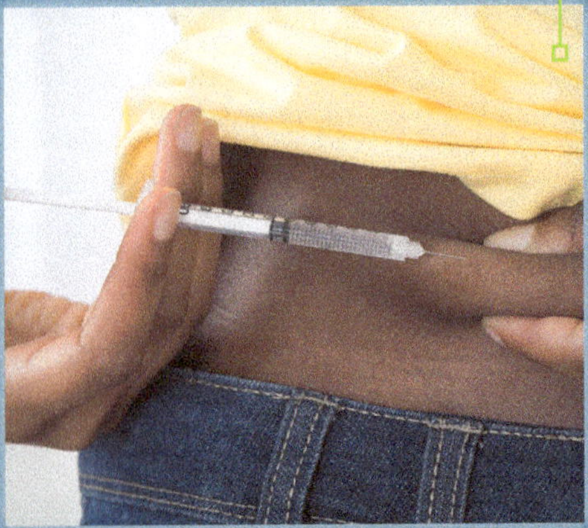

People with diabetes use injections to control the amount of sugar in their blood.

Spiders spin silk to make webs. The silk might have many uses—if it can be made in large quantities.

UNANSWERED

Some scientists hope genetic engineering may make it possible to "recreate" extinct animals. For example, the Quagga Project aims to breed the extinct horselike quagga from its living relative, the plains zebra. So far, the process has only produced plains zebra that look like quagga. However, artificial selection and cloning technology may eventually make it possible to use preserved quagga DNA to breed what would be new individuals of the lost species.

GM technology also helps produce food. Scientists have modified crops to make them resistant to diseases or harsh conditions. Some plants are designed to resist weed killers. Farmers plant GM seeds, like soybeans and corn, and treat their fields with a weed killer made by the same company. The crop survives the weed killer, but all other plants die. The results of GM crops are mixed, however. Many countries do not allow GM crops.

Scientists have also produced GM animals, such as the spider-silk goat. Spider silk is very strong but lightweight, and has many properties that engineers hope to put to use. However, spiders do not produce silk in large amounts. Spider genes have been added to GM goats so they produce liquid silk proteins in their milk, which can then be extracted as silk.

-CHAPTER 4-

GENE THERAPY

Everything about us is due to our genes: our eye color, hair type, height, and even our personality and intelligence. Although genes have an impact on these things, geneticists have not found all the sections of human DNA that control them. They also don't know how the DNA code translates into each characteristic. Decoding the human genome is still in its early days—there is a long way to go.

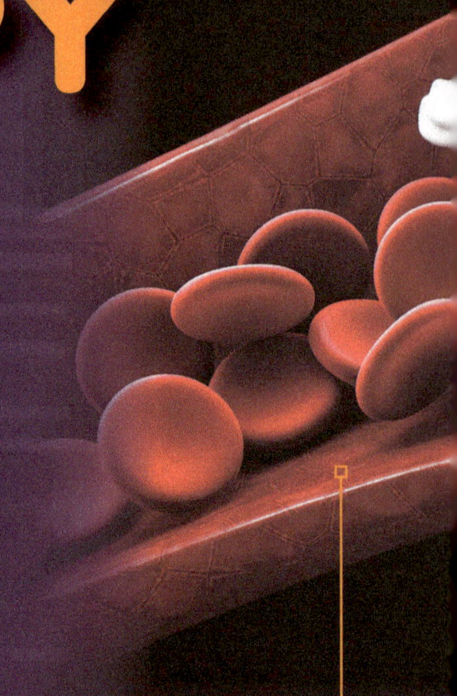

Sickle cell anemia damages blood cells (right of center), blocking the blood vessels.

Most research efforts concentrate on finding genes that cause diseases. Geneticists have had some success. They have isolated the genes that cause disorders such as the blood diseases sickle cell anemia and hemophilia. In sickle cell anemia, blood cells are curved so they do not carry oxygen properly and may block up small blood vessels. In hemophilia, the blood cannot form scabs that seal up wounds.

Such diseases are usually treated using drugs. Gene therapy sets out to fix the problem by changing the faulty gene that causes the disease. It seems likely that gene therapy will change the way medicine works—but not just yet. Getting the new gene into the body instead of the old one is proving a difficult process.

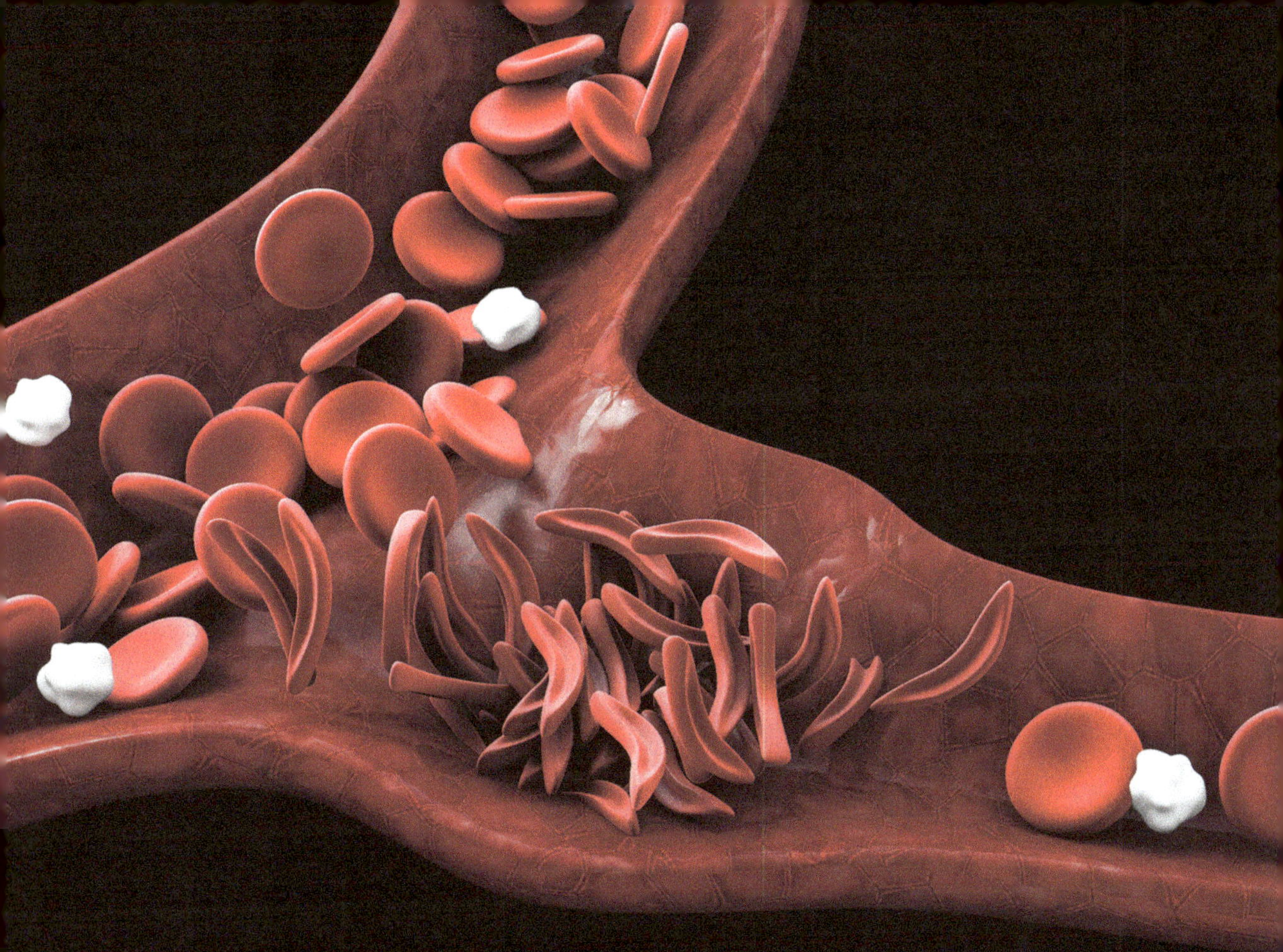

DNA can be injected straight into the body of someone with a disease, but this has little impact. The faulty tissue could be targeted with a GM virus that adds a fix. However, the cells in the rest of the body would still carry the bad gene—meaning it could be passed on to the next generation.

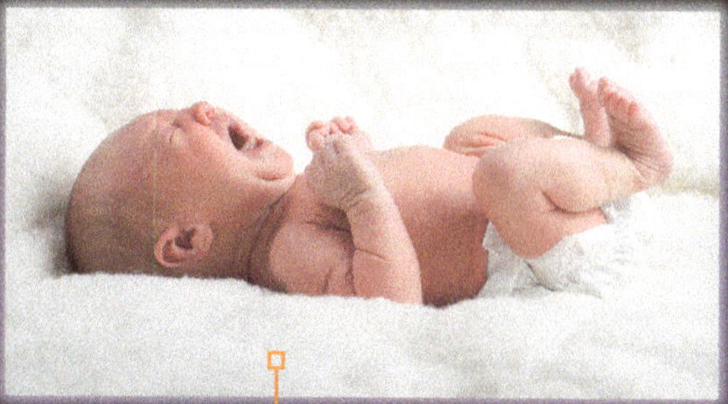

Might parents choose to create a baby that never cried?

Some gene therapies focus on preventing a child from inheriting a disease. This involves screening unborn offspring or even altering genes in sperm or eggs. However, some critics argue that if we start editing a baby's genes, parents may eventually want to change things that are not linked to their child's health at all.

REPLACE AND RENEW

One of the most exciting fields of genetic therapy involves using stem cells. Stem-cell therapy uses the body's own systems to repair body parts that are damaged by disease or just worn out by old age.

The human body is good at repairing itself, but it cannot heal all forms of damage. For example, if nerve cells are severed, they cannot grow back again. In most cases, this results in some kind of permanent damage. Similarly, while the skin and other organs can repair and regenerate, they cannot always heal fully if they are badly damaged.

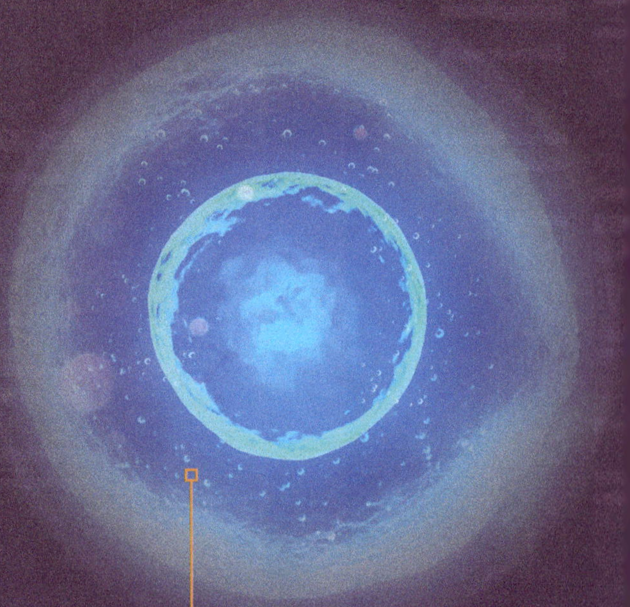

It might be possible to use stem cells to help the body heal itself.

Genetics researchers are using stem cells to try to fix these problems. These cells, which have the capacity to differentiate into a whole range of cells, are not only present in a young, growing body. They are also still active in many parts of the adult body, such as the stomach lining, the genitals, and the bone marrow, which is the soft center inside large bones. Bone marrow constantly manufactures new blood cells, and bone marrow transplants are one of the simplest forms of stem-cell therapy.

UNANSWERED

The cloning system that created Dolly the Sheep turned a specialized body cell into a stem cell that could differentiate into a whole range of cells. As this kind of cell develops into an embryo, it produces all the stem cells needed to make a body—and to fix it, too. Will we one day clone ourselves and harvest tiny embryo versions of ourselves to fix problems with our bodies? It sounds horrible—but what if it could save your life? You might think differently.

Blood diseases such as leukemia are caused by problems with cells made in bone marrow. Scientists fix the problem by killing the bone marrow and transplanting in healthy cells from someone else.

The major goal of stem-cell research is to find ways of reprogramming cells so they can be used to rebuild any body tissue, not just the few for which the body already makes them, such as bone marrow. To do that, geneticists must find a way to unlock the genes hidden away inside every cell.

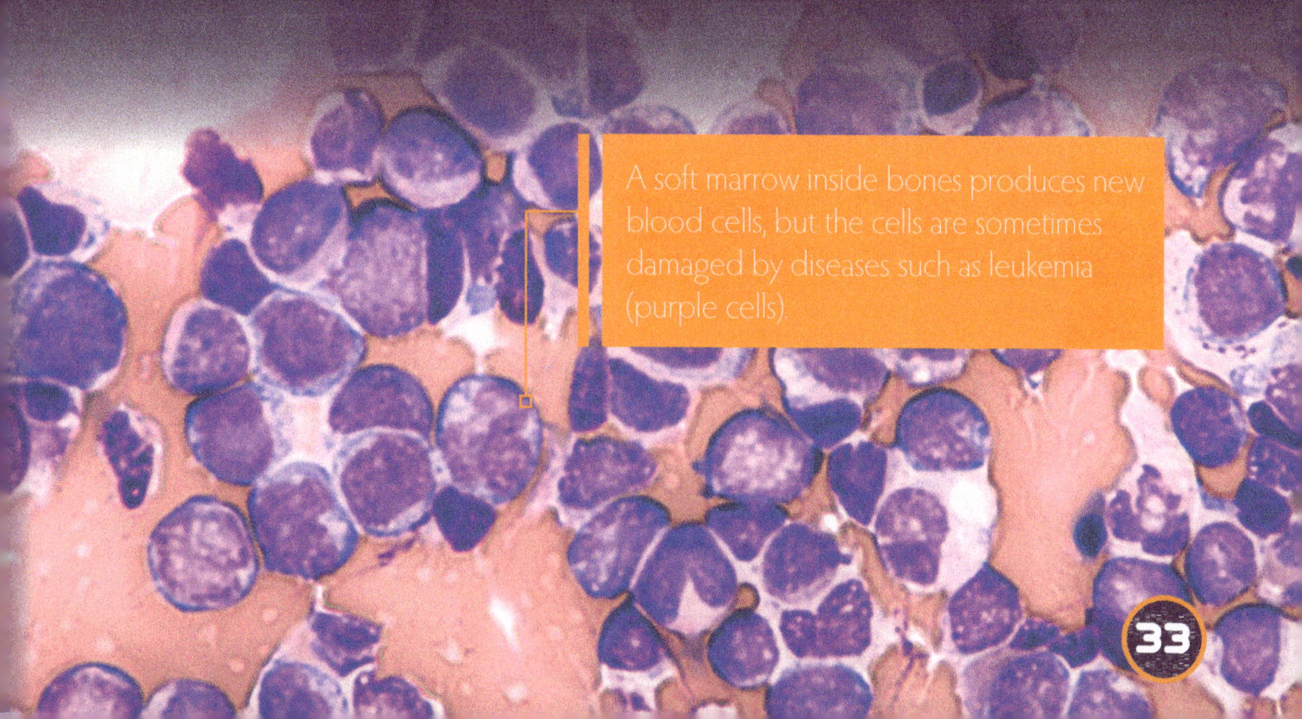

A soft marrow inside bones produces new blood cells, but the cells are sometimes damaged by diseases such as leukemia (purple cells).

CHAPTER 5

SUPERHUMANS

Science has given humans at least some control over our genes and the problems they cause us. That leads some people to wonder if the human species will continue to evolve. In the past, people with gene-based diseases died younger and had fewer children than healthy people. The genes they carried would become less common among the human population. In contrast, stronger genes that helped rather than hindered survival would become more common. That was natural selection in operation.

Will everyone become a superhuman?

Advances in medicine, combined with humans' ability to grow food and create places to live, has reduced the impact of natural selection. Does that mean that humans will stop evolving? Evolution by natural selection is such a slow process compared to the human lifespan that it is impossible to tell—but experts believe the answer is probably no.

If humans do continue to evolve, this does not mean that the whole human race will evolve into something else. However, there might be a likelihood that humanity might divide into two or more species—and genetic technology might be why.

Scientists using gene therapies are beginning to modify the genes of humans. Today they do this largely to cure diseases and other conditions. But what if experts were to discover genes that would make people stronger, smarter, and more attractive? Why would people not want those genes, too? Perhaps genetic engineers could design brand-new genes that gave us superpowers—so we could see heat rays as a snake does, hear as well as an owl, or go into a deep sleep like a mouse while we make long space journeys.

Only a few people would ever be able to afford personalized genetic modifications like this. Once they were modified, they might not be able to have children with non-GM people—and even if they could, they might not want to. As a result, they would grow apart from "ordinary" humans to form part of a new species. Some people suggest superhumans like this are only a few decades away—but only if humanity decides to allow their creation.

The journey to distant planets could take decades, so astronauts might need to **hibernate** on the way.

EUGENICS

Genetic modification of humans could have many benefits—but it would certainly cause misery, too. The twentieth century was the bloodiest period of human history. More than 100 million people died in warfare. The largest and most costly war of all was World War II (1939–1945). The war was caused in large part by fascism, a political system popular in Germany and Italy. Fascism was based on genetics. The Nazis in Germany believed that people who shared "good" genes—tall, blonde, northern Europeans—were superior to other humans and should rule the world.

The Nazi leader Adolf Hitler wanted to create an "ideal" race of young Germans.

This idea was inspired by the work of the nineteenth-century British mathematician Francis Galton. (Galton also happened to be the brother-in-law of Charles Darwin, who first proposed the theory of evolution through natural selection.) Galton's idea was called **eugenics**. He suggested that the human race should artificially breed itself to become smarter and better. Galton began measuring people, especially their heads, to try to figure out what these "smart and better" people looked like.

BEHIND THE THEORY

Francis Galton is best remembered for his unethical genetic ideas. He also made other contributions to science. He came up with the idea of the Wisdom of Crowds, in which it is possible to make an accurate estimate of a quantity by asking many people to guess it. Even if no one guesses right, the average of all the guesses will be very close to the true answer. Galton also showed that the chance of two people having the same fingerprint was so low that fingerprints could be used for identification.

Then, Galton suggested, people who fit these ideal measurements would be allowed to breed together—but no one else.

Galton's idea failed because he could not discover any link between the way someone looked and whether or not they were smarter or morally "better." However, if a race of GM humans were ever to be created, there would be clear evidence in their DNA that they were different from us. Would that make it okay for them to rule the world?

Every fingerprint has a unique identity.

-CHAPTER 6-

GENETICS IN THE FUTURE

Geneticists still face many challenges. Since the days of Gregor Mendel, they have figured out more and more about the way in which the DNA code in the genotype turns into observable phenotypes. The process turns out to be much more complicated than the simple system of dominant and recessive alleles. Genes sometimes team up as "supergenes," which turn other genes on or off, for example. Recent discoveries suggest that a completely separate system controls which genes are allowed to work in a cell. This idea is being probed by a new branch of science known as epigenetics.

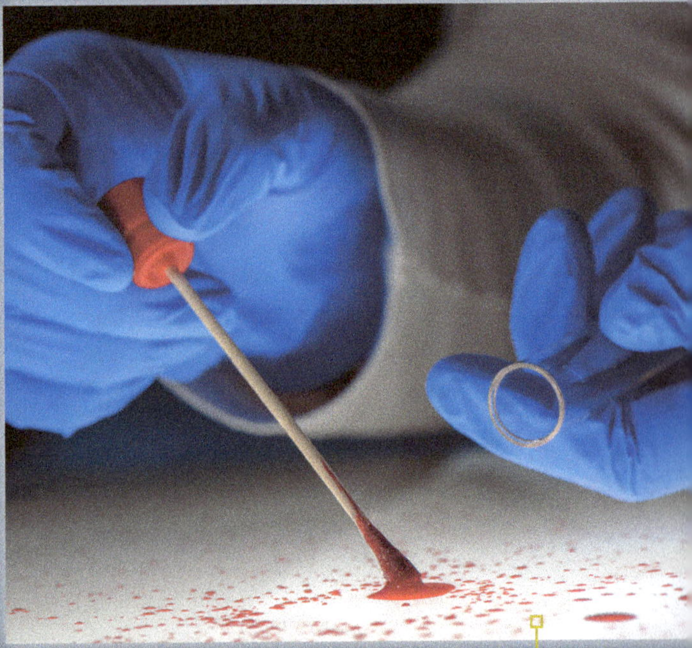

Detectives gather blood samples at a crime scene to analyze their DNA in the hopes of using it to identify the criminal.

Bioengineers are exploring the way life uses DNA and genes to build bodies and control complex systems. They are already copying from nature in order to build entirely new forms of life.

In the future, older forms of genetic technology will also become cheaper, faster, and easier. For example, the police often use DNA fingerprinting, or profiling. In this technique, investigators use DNA evidence taken from a crime scene to match that of a suspect. The process takes a minimum of about 24 hours to complete—but often much longer. New electronic technology only needs tiny amounts of DNA to analyze. This new technology has shortened the process to just four hours—and it will rapidly become even faster.

DNA fingerprints do not map all of a person's DNA. They focus on any unusual features in their code, such as sections that repeat one "letter" over and over. These act as markers that can be compared to those from another sample. If they match, then the DNA comes from the same person—or someone closely related to them.

Some people also use DNA tests to examine their romantic relationships. These tests work in the opposite way from DNA fingerprints. They look for differences rather than similarities in DNA in the system the body uses to identify its own cells. Heterosexual people are often attracted to members of the opposite sex where this system is wildly different—they appear to be alerted by their mate's smell. If these systems are different, many of the individuals' other genes will be, too. Combining different genes makes for healthy babies. Perhaps attraction between genetically diverse people has a biological benefit for the process of human reproduction?

Comparing sets of DNA can produce a match—or highlight any differences.

EPIGENETICS

Geneticists have always believed that information from the genes cannot be altered by the body. In other words, inherited information is not changed by the actions of an organism. However, a new concept called epigenetics—"on top of genetics"—is challenging that rule.

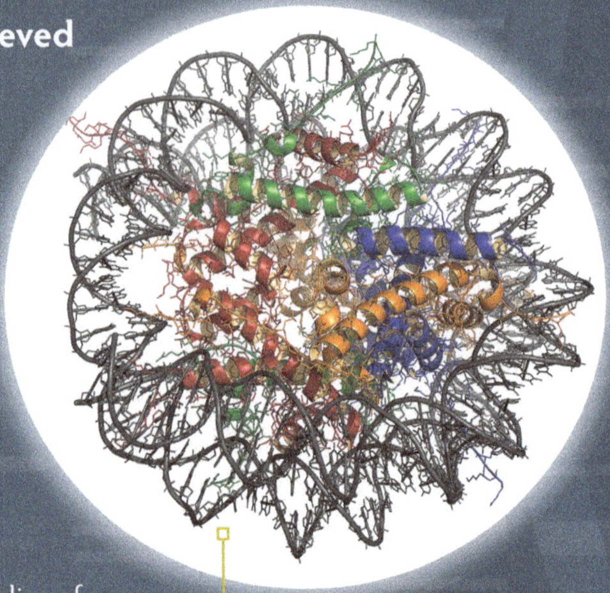

Some genetic information may be carried outside molecules of DNA.

This field arose from large-scale studies of famine victims in World War II. Children born during the famine were small because their mothers did not have enough to eat as they developed in the womb. Children born a few months after the famine were normal size. They had started developing during the famine, but grew rapidly once their mothers' food supply returned. The group born during the famine stayed small and thin their whole lives. The second group struggled with obesity and were likely to suffer from mental illnesses. The children and grandchildren of this second group also had the same issues. It is too early to tell if their great-grandchildren will have the same issues, too. This discovery suggests that although the famine did not change the children's genes, it changed how the genes worked. Researchers began to study the epigenome to learn more.

BEHIND THE THEORY

The idea of epigenetics is similar to the ideas of the nineteenth-century French scientist Jean-Baptiste Lamarck. Lamarck proposed a theory of evolution 60 years before Charles Darwin. Lamarck suggested that the attributes an organism acquired during its life were passed on to the next generation. For example, a giraffe developed a long neck because it had to stretch to reach leaves in tall trees. Its offspring were born with longer, pre-stretched necks—and giraffes evolved to be taller and taller.

The epigenome are proteins and other chemicals in a chromosome that fold and coil around the DNA molecule. It seems that events during life—like the famine—change the epigenome. It locks away some genes and unfolds others for the cell to use. The epigenetic changes of the famine were passed on through the generations. Researchers are studying how the epigenome changes during a lifetime. If they figure out how it works, this may help in understanding everything from stem cells to the impact of lifestyle on health.

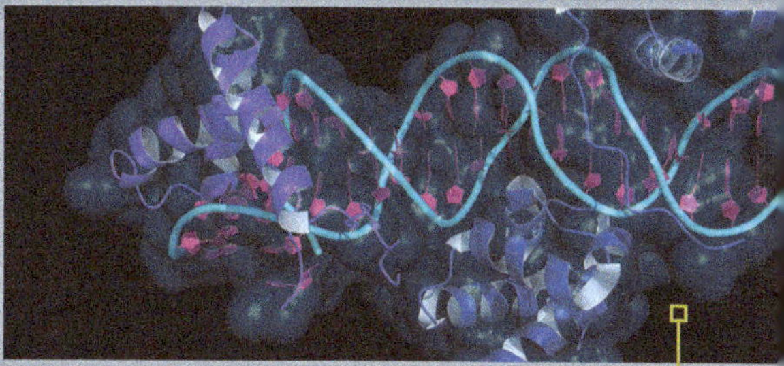

Is there a means by which changes during a person's life can affect their genes?

XNA AND XENOBIOLOGY

Xenobiology, or "strange biology," is a new field of science. It aims to build new forms of life that are not based on DNA but on artificial molecules called XNA (xenonucleic acid). DNA is good at carrying genes, but it needs looking after and can be easily damaged. The different types of XNA copy how DNA works and use the same letter-based code—but they are made from tougher stuff.

An organism that uses XNA might be able to survive in harsh environments filled with poisons or dangerous temperatures. They could even live on other planets. If a form of XNA could be used in gene therapies, it might gradually replace human DNA to make people immune to toxins and **radioactivity**.

Will developments in biology make it possible to replace human DNA?

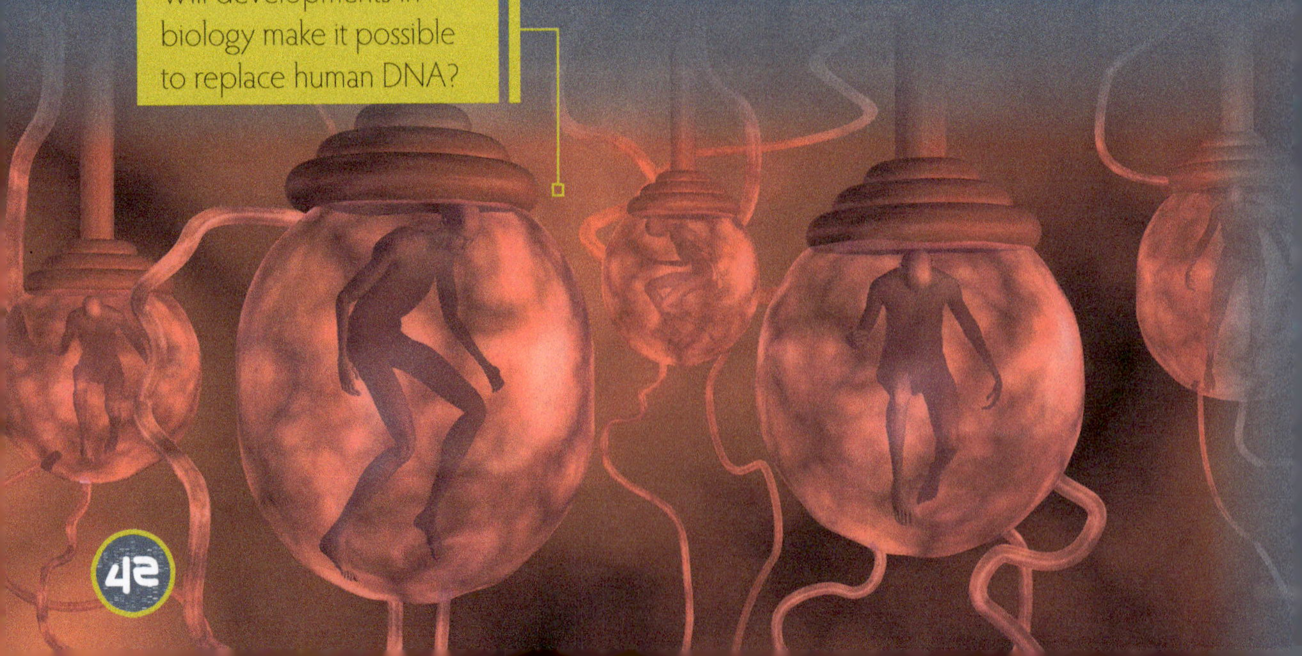

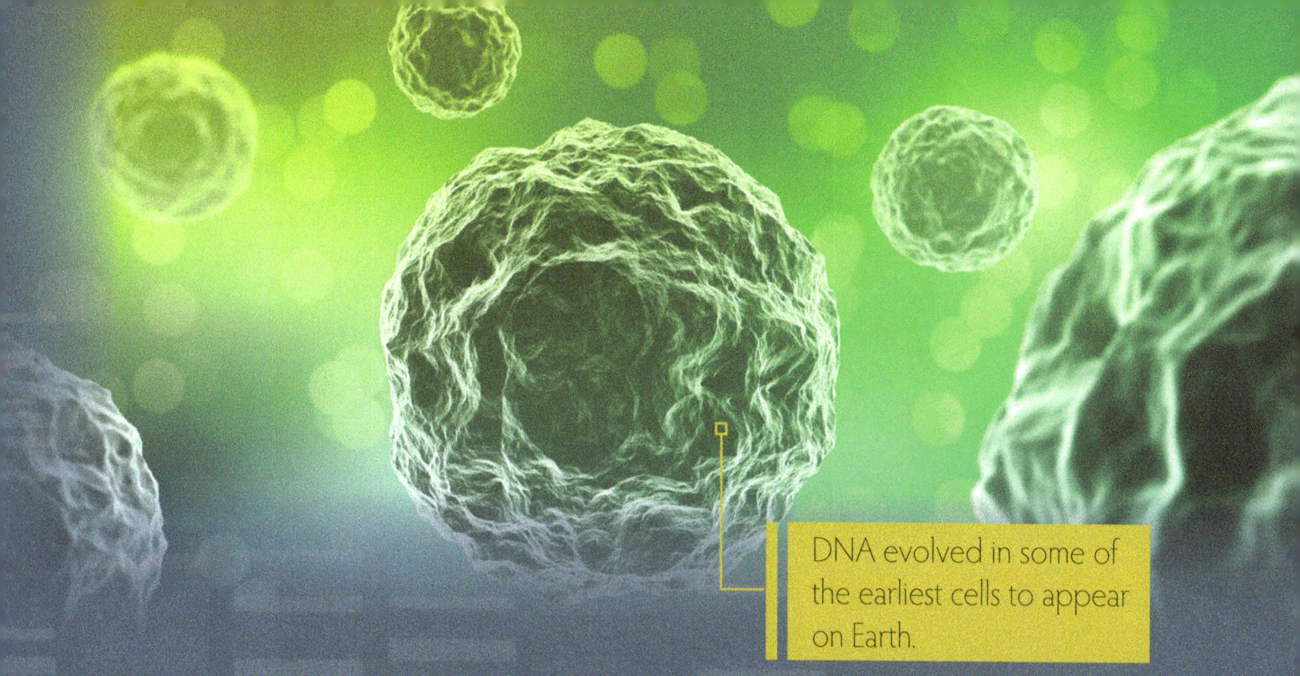

DNA evolved in some of the earliest cells to appear on Earth.

XNA and xenobiology are part of a wider field called synthetic biology. This is where scientists use biological structures, such as enzymes, membranes, and DNA, to assemble new life forms. Currently, they have succeeded in using parts taken from bacteria and putting them together with an artificial set of genes. Adding XNA and other nonbiological materials that copy natural ones might one day create an entirely new form of life. Perhaps the robots of the future will not be made from plastic and metals but will be grown using synthetic biology. After many centuries, humans are still using genetics to change the nature of life itself. The power of the gene is only just beginning to be fully understood.

UNANSWERED

XNAs are based on chemicals researchers discovered while investigating how DNA became so central to life. Current theories suggest that DNA evolved from a soup of simpler chemicals that formed in the warm chemical-rich environment of the early Earth. DNA and its cousin, RNA, were likely so good at building copies of their own molecules that other compounds could not compete and eventually disappeared.

TIMELINE

10,000 BC Humans begin to breed wild plants to make them more useful.

1809 French scientist Jean-Baptiste Lamarck suggests that animals acquire characteristics that they pass on to their offspring.

1859 The English scientist Charles Darwin outlines a theory of evolution by what he calls natural selection.

1865 The Czech monk Gregor Mendel experiments with pea plants and figures out that parents transmit information to their offspring through distinct units. This is the start of gene theory.

1869 Swiss researcher Friedrich Miescher separates DNA from cells.

1883 English scientist Francis Galton invents the word "eugenics" to describe his program to "improve" humans through selective breeding.

1900 A growing understanding of cells and chromosomes encourages researchers to reconsider the theories of Gregor Mendel.

1909 The Danish scientist Wilhelm Johannsen invents the word "gene" to describe the units that carry information from parents to their offspring.

1911 US researchers discover that genes are carried on chromosomes.

1941 US scientists show that genes control chemicals inside cells.

1944 The US scientist Oswald Avery identifies DNA as the method by which genes cause changes in organisms.

1950 US scientist Erwin Chargaff figures out that each living species has its own DNA.

1952 British reseachers Rosalind Franklin and Raymond Gosling photograph fibers of DNA.

1953 In Cambridge, England, James Watson and Francis Crick discover the double-helix structure of DNA.

1955 Indonesian-born US scientist Joe Hin Tjio defines the number of chromosomes in the human cell as 46.

1959 Researchers discover that Down Syndrome is caused by a fault with a specific chromosome.

1966 Researchers figure out the genetic code that allows the four nucleic bases to order the 20 amino acids in proteins.

1973 Researchers clone the first animal genes, using frogs.

1990 The Human Genome Project is launched as a 15-year program to sequence all 3.2 billion letters of the human genome.

1994 The Food and Drug Administration (FDA) approves the first genetically modified food, the Flavr Savr tomato.

1996 The first large mammal is cloned, Dolly the Sheep.

2003 The complete human genome is sequenced.

2012 Governments and other official bodies begin to consider the implications of the new field of xenobiology.

2013 Scientists discover that identical twins have small genetic differences.

GLOSSARY

alleles different forms of the same gene

asexually taking place without male and female parents

bilaterally symmetrical with one side directly echoing the other

blastocyst a cluster of cells at an early stage of reproduction

cells the units that make up living things

chromosomes threadlike structures that carry genes in the nucleus of cells

cistron a section of DNA or RNA code

clones organisms that are genetically identical to their parents

differentiate to become different during development

epigenetics relating to non-genetic influences on genetics

ethical related to right or wrong behavior

eugenics using controlled breeding to make changes to a population

extinction a situation in which a species no longer exists

genome the complete set of DNA of an organism

genotype the genetic makeup of an individual

hibernate to spend a long period in a sleeplike state

hormone a substance that controls the actions of cells in the body

mitochondria parts of a cell that produce energy

molecule a group of cells joined together

natural selection the process by which organisms better suited to their environment survive and produce more young, changing a species over time

organs self-contained parts of the body with specific functions, such as the heart

phenotype the observable characteristics of an individual

potent having the ability to become different cells

primates the group of mammals that includes humans, monkeys, and apes

proteins molecules that make up body tissues

radioactivity a stream of energy from disintegrating atoms

ribosome a minute particle of protein

sex cells cells that enable reproduction. A male cell is a sperm, and a female cell is an egg

species a related group of living things

synthetic made artificially

transplantation moving an organ or another part of the body from one individual to another

tumor an unusual growth inside the body

uterus the place where young develop inside a mother

zygote the cell formed by two sex cells during reproduction

FOR MORE INFORMATION

BOOKS

Bond, Dave. *Genetic Engineering*. Broomall, PA: Mason Crest, 2017.

Colson, Mary. *GMOs*. New York, NY: Gareth Stevens Publishing, 2016.

Henneberg, Susan (ed.). *Genetic Engineering*. New York, NY: Greenhaven Press, 2017.

Jackson, Tom. *Genetics: Why We Are Who We Are*. New York, NY: Cavendish Square Publishing, 2017.

Jennings, Cecilia. *DNA Evidence: The Proof Is in the Genes*. New York, NY: Lucent Books, 2018.

WEBSITES

science.howstuffworks.com/life/genetic/cloning.htm
A page from How Stuff Works explaining the process of creating clones, including the story of Dolly the Sheep.

encyclopedia.kids.net.au/page/ge/Gene_therapy
A Kids Net page about using genes to treat disease and other conditions.

science.lovetoknow.com/genetics-kids
A Fun With Science introduction to genetics.

www.ducksters.com/science/biology/mendel_and_inheritance.php
This page from Ducksters explains how Gregor Mendel laid the foundations for the understanding of inheritance.

Publisher's note to educators and parents: Our editors have carefully reviewed these websites to ensure that they are suitable for students. Many websites change frequently, however, and we cannot guarantee that a site's future contents will continue to meet our high standards of quality and educational value. Be advised that students should be closely supervised whenever they access the Internet.

INDEX